The Internet of Things:
Connecting the World Around Us

By

Brad M. Davis

TABLE OF CONTENTS

Introduction

A. Definition of the Internet of Things (IoT)

The world we live in is becoming increasingly interconnected, thanks to the rapid advancements in technology. One of the most transformative and revolutionary developments in recent times is the Internet of Things (IoT). The IoT refers to a vast network of interconnected devices, objects, and systems that communicate with each other and share data over the internet. It encompasses a wide range of objects, including everyday items such as smart appliances, wearable devices, industrial machinery, and even entire smart cities.

At its core, the Internet of Things represents the convergence of physical and digital realms, where objects in the physical world are seamlessly integrated into the digital ecosystem. These objects, often embedded with sensors and actuators, have the ability to collect and transmit data, interact with their environment, and respond to commands or triggers. This interconnectedness enables a new level of automation, efficiency, and convenience in various aspects of our lives.

The scope of the IoT is vast and ever-expanding. It has the potential to revolutionize multiple industries, including healthcare, transportation, manufacturing, agriculture, and more. By connecting devices and systems, the IoT enables us to gather valuable insights, automate processes, improve decision-making, and enhance overall productivity and quality of life.

This book, "The Internet of Things: Connecting the World Around Us," aims to provide a comprehensive understanding of the IoT landscape. It explores the technologies that enable IoT, the core components of IoT systems, and the diverse range of applications across various sectors. Additionally, it delves into the challenges and considerations associated with IoT, such as security, privacy, interoperability, and ethical implications.

Throughout the book, readers will gain insights into the historical evolution of IoT, the underlying technologies, and the transformative potential of connected devices.

By examining real-world use cases and industry examples, readers will discover the practical applications and benefits of IoT in different contexts. Moreover, the book will address the challenges and risks associated with IoT deployment, while also discussing future trends and possibilities.

As the world becomes increasingly interconnected, it is crucial to grasp the fundamentals of the Internet of Things. By understanding its definition, components, applications, and implications, readers will be equipped to navigate the connected world and make informed decisions in a rapidly evolving technological landscape. Let's embark on a journey to explore the fascinating realm of the Internet of Things and its profound impact on our lives.

B. Importance and scope of IoT in today's world

In today's rapidly evolving digital landscape, the Internet of Things (IoT) has emerged as a pivotal force that is reshaping the way we interact with technology and the world around us. The importance and scope of IoT in our lives cannot be overstated, as it holds immense potential to revolutionize industries, enhance efficiency, and improve the overall quality of life.

At its core, the IoT connects physical objects and devices to the internet, enabling them to gather and share data, communicate, and collaborate. This interconnectedness creates a vast ecosystem of smart devices, sensors, actuators, and systems that work in harmony to collect, analyze, and act upon data. The implications of this technology stretch across various domains, from everyday consumer applications to complex industrial processes.

The importance of IoT lies in its ability to generate vast amounts of data from diverse sources, enabling organizations and individuals to gain valuable insights into operations, environments, and behaviors. This data-driven approach empowers businesses to make data-backed decisions, optimize processes, and deliver enhanced products and services. Additionally, IoT facilitates real-time monitoring, predictive maintenance, and automation, leading to increased efficiency, reduced costs, and improved safety in industrial settings.

Beyond the industrial sector, IoT has permeated into our daily lives, transforming the way we interact with our homes, cities, and personal devices. Smart homes equipped with IoT-enabled devices provide convenience, security, and energy efficiency through automated systems for lighting, temperature control, and security monitoring. In smart cities, IoT plays a vital role in managing urban infrastructures, optimizing traffic flow, reducing energy consumption, and enhancing public safety.

The scope of IoT is expanding rapidly, with innovative applications emerging in areas such as healthcare, agriculture, transportation, and environmental monitoring. In healthcare, IoT devices and wearables enable remote patient monitoring, personalized healthcare, and early detection of health issues. In agriculture, IoT-based systems aid in precision farming, optimizing irrigation, and monitoring crop health. Transportation systems benefit from IoT by enabling real-time tracking, route optimization, and predictive maintenance for vehicles.

However, with the ever-increasing number of connected devices, the scope of IoT also brings forth challenges and considerations. Security and privacy are major concerns, as a breach in IoT systems can have severe consequences. Interoperability among different IoT devices and the need for standardized protocols also pose challenges. Furthermore, ethical considerations arise regarding data ownership, privacy, and the potential impact of IoT on employment and society as a whole.

In conclusion, the importance and scope of IoT in today's world are undeniable. It has the potential to transform industries, enhance productivity, and improve our daily lives. Understanding the fundamental concepts, applications, and challenges associated with IoT is crucial for individuals, businesses, and policymakers to harness its transformative power responsibly. By exploring the multifaceted dimensions of IoT, this book aims to provide readers with a comprehensive understanding of this groundbreaking technology and its impact on the world around us.

C. Overview of the book's purpose and structure

"The Internet of Things: Connecting the World Around Us" is a comprehensive guide that aims to provide readers with a deep understanding of the Internet of Things (IoT) and its transformative impact on our interconnected world. This book serves as a roadmap for both beginners and professionals seeking to explore the intricacies of IoT, its applications, challenges, and future possibilities.

The purpose of this book is to offer a holistic overview of the IoT landscape, delving into its definition, core components, and diverse applications across industries. It is designed to equip readers with the knowledge and insights necessary to navigate the dynamic world of IoT and harness its potential to drive innovation and create positive change.

The structure of the book is organized into logical sections, each exploring different facets of IoT. It begins with an introduction that provides a clear definition of the IoT and establishes its importance and scope in today's world. This section sets the stage for readers to understand the subsequent chapters and grasp the significance of IoT in various domains.

The book then delves into the evolution of IoT, tracing its historical origins and examining the technological advancements that have paved the way for its rapid growth. By exploring the past, readers gain a deeper appreciation for the present and a better understanding of the forces shaping the future of IoT.

The core components of IoT are explored in detail, with a focus on sensors and actuators, connectivity, and data management and analytics. This section highlights the fundamental building blocks that enable the seamless communication and interaction between IoT devices and systems. Readers will gain insights into the types of sensors and their functionalities, wireless communication protocols, network infrastructures, data collection, storage, and analytics techniques.

The book then delves into the myriad applications of IoT across different sectors. From smart homes and home automation to industrial IoT (IIoT), smart cities, and healthcare, readers will explore real-world use cases and understand how IoT is revolutionizing these industries. Each application is examined in terms of its benefits, challenges, and potential for further innovation.

Challenges and considerations in the realm of IoT are also addressed in this book. Security and privacy, interoperability, and ethical and social implications are discussed in-depth, shedding light on the potential risks and concerns associated with the widespread adoption of IoT. Understanding these challenges is crucial for ensuring responsible and secure implementation of IoT technologies.

The book concludes with a visionary outlook on the future of IoT. Emerging trends, such as the integration of artificial intelligence (AI) and machine learning, edge computing, fog computing, and the impact of 5G and next-generation networks, are explored. By examining these future possibilities, readers gain valuable insights into the direction in which IoT is heading and the potential disruptions it may bring.

In summary, "The Internet of Things: Connecting the World Around Us" offers a comprehensive overview of IoT, its applications, challenges, and future prospects. With its structured approach and accessible language, this book serves as a valuable resource for anyone interested in understanding and harnessing the power of IoT in our increasingly interconnected world.

CHAPTER II
The Evolution of IoT

A. Historical background and origins of IoT

The concept of the Internet of Things (IoT) has its roots in early visions of a connected world, where physical objects could communicate and interact with each other and with humans. The foundations of IoT can be traced back several decades, with notable milestones and developments that have paved the way for its current state.

The origins of IoT can be attributed to the field of embedded systems, where devices with limited computing power and connectivity were integrated into various applications. The term "Internet of Things" was coined in 1999 by British technology pioneer Kevin Ashton, who recognized the potential of connecting everyday objects to the internet. This marked a significant turning point in the conceptualization of IoT as a revolutionary idea.

In the early 2000s, researchers and innovators began exploring the possibilities of IoT on a larger scale. The convergence of wireless communication, sensors, and the internet laid the groundwork for IoT's expansion. One of the first major IoT projects was the Auto-ID Center at the Massachusetts Institute of Technology (MIT), which aimed to develop technologies for tracking and identifying objects using radio frequency identification (RFID) tags.

As technology advanced, the vision of a truly interconnected world gained traction. The proliferation of smartphones and the widespread availability of high-speed internet created an environment conducive to the growth of IoT. With the increasing number of devices capable of connecting to the internet, the potential for IoT applications expanded exponentially.

Industries such as healthcare, transportation, and manufacturing started incorporating IoT solutions to improve efficiency and enhance operations. The healthcare sector, for example, began utilizing IoT devices for remote patient monitoring and telehealth services, enabling healthcare providers to deliver personalized care and monitor patients' well-being remotely.

The advent of smart homes and wearable devices further propelled the IoT revolution. Home automation systems equipped with IoT technologies allowed users to control and monitor various aspects of their homes, including lighting, security, and energy consumption, through connected devices and voice assistants. Wearable devices, such as fitness trackers and smartwatches, became increasingly popular, collecting data about users' health and fitness levels.

Today, IoT has permeated nearly every aspect of our lives, from our homes and workplaces to our cities and public infrastructure. The advancements in cloud computing, edge computing, and data analytics have further accelerated the capabilities of IoT. The ability to collect, process, and analyze massive amounts of data in real-time has unlocked new possibilities for improving efficiency, enhancing decision-making, and creating innovative services.

Looking ahead, the evolution of IoT continues with the integration of artificial intelligence (AI) and machine learning. AI-powered IoT systems can autonomously analyze and interpret data, make intelligent decisions, and adapt to changing circumstances. This convergence of IoT and AI opens up new frontiers, enabling predictive maintenance, personalized experiences, and more efficient resource allocation.

In conclusion, the historical background and origins of IoT can be traced back to visionary thinkers and pioneers who recognized the potential of connecting objects to the internet. From its inception to the present day, IoT has undergone significant evolution, driven by advancements in technology, connectivity, and data analytics. The journey of IoT continues, pushing the boundaries of innovation and transforming the way we interact with the world around us.

B. Technological Advancements Enabling IoT

The evolution of the Internet of Things (IoT) has been propelled by numerous technological advancements that have enabled the seamless connectivity and integration of a wide array of devices and systems. These advancements have played a vital role in shaping the development and expansion of IoT as we know it today.

One of the key technological enablers of IoT is wireless communication. The advent of wireless networking technologies, such as Wi-Fi, Bluetooth, and cellular networks, has eliminated the need for physical connections between devices, making it easier to connect and communicate with IoT devices. This wireless connectivity has opened up a realm of possibilities for IoT applications, allowing devices to transmit and receive data without constraints.

Another crucial advancement is the miniaturization of electronic components. Smaller and more powerful microprocessors, sensors, and actuators have made it feasible to embed computing capabilities into everyday objects, transforming them into IoT devices. These compact components consume less power, are cost-effective, and can be integrated seamlessly into various environments, contributing to the proliferation of IoT.

The development of low-power technologies has also been instrumental in the growth of IoT. Battery life is a crucial consideration for IoT devices, as many of them are designed to operate for extended periods without the need for frequent battery replacements. Energy-efficient protocols and low-power processors enable IoT devices to conserve energy and prolong their battery life, facilitating their deployment in diverse applications, ranging from smart homes to remote monitoring systems.

Cloud computing has revolutionized the storage and processing capabilities of IoT systems. By leveraging the power of the cloud, IoT devices can offload data storage and computational tasks to remote servers, eliminating the need for extensive local processing capabilities. Cloud computing provides scalable and on-demand resources, allowing IoT systems to handle the massive amounts of data generated by interconnected devices and facilitating real-time analytics and insights.

Advancements in data analytics and machine learning have been pivotal in unlocking the value of IoT-generated data. The ability to extract meaningful insights from vast volumes of data has empowered businesses to make data-driven decisions, optimize operations, and enhance user experiences. Machine learning algorithms applied to IoT data enable predictive maintenance, anomaly detection, and personalized services, augmenting the capabilities of IoT systems and unlocking new opportunities for innovation.

Furthermore, edge computing has emerged as a critical technological paradigm in the IoT landscape. Edge computing involves performing computation and data processing closer to the source of data generation, reducing latency and enhancing real-time decision-making. By processing data at the edge of the network, IoT devices can respond quickly to events, minimize bandwidth usage, and address privacy and security concerns associated with transmitting sensitive data to the cloud.

Looking ahead, emerging technologies such as 5G, with its higher bandwidth and lower latency, will further propel the growth of IoT by enabling faster and more reliable communication between devices. Additionally, advancements in blockchain technology hold promise for enhancing the security, privacy, and trust in IoT systems by providing decentralized and tamper-resistant data storage and transactions.

In conclusion, technological advancements have played a pivotal role in the evolution and proliferation of IoT. Wireless communication, miniaturization of components, low-power technologies, cloud computing, data analytics, machine learning, edge computing, and upcoming technologies like 5G and blockchain have collectively driven the growth and potential of IoT. These advancements have transformed everyday objects into smart and interconnected devices, revolutionizing industries, improving efficiency, and enhancing our quality of life in the increasingly interconnected world of IoT.

C. Examples of Early IoT Applications

As the Internet of Things (IoT) has evolved, numerous early applications have paved the way for its widespread adoption and integration into various industries. These pioneering examples showcase the transformative potential of IoT and highlight how interconnected devices can enhance efficiency, productivity, and convenience.

One of the earliest and most notable applications of IoT is in the field of healthcare. Remote patient monitoring systems enabled by IoT have revolutionized healthcare delivery by allowing healthcare providers to monitor patients' vital signs and health conditions remotely. IoT-enabled wearable devices, such as smartwatches and fitness trackers, track individuals' physical activities, heart rate, and sleep patterns, providing valuable data for personalized healthcare and preventive measures.

In the transportation sector, early IoT applications focused on improving efficiency and safety. Fleet management systems equipped with IoT technologies enabled real-time tracking of vehicles, optimizing routes, monitoring fuel consumption, and enhancing logistics operations. IoT-based telematics systems collected and analyzed data from sensors embedded in vehicles, providing insights for preventive maintenance, reducing downtime, and improving overall safety on the roads.

The concept of smart homes emerged as an early IoT application, transforming the way we interact with our living spaces. IoT-enabled devices, such as smart thermostats, lighting systems, and security cameras, offered homeowners the ability to remotely control and monitor various aspects of their homes through mobile apps or voice assistants. These early IoT applications paved the way for the proliferation of smart home devices and the creation of interconnected ecosystems that enhance comfort, energy efficiency, and security.

In the industrial sector, IoT found early applications in optimizing manufacturing processes and asset management. Industrial IoT (IIoT) systems utilized sensors and connectivity to monitor machinery, collect real-time data, and facilitate predictive maintenance. This enabled proactive repairs, reduced downtime, and improved overall equipment efficiency. IIoT also provided valuable insights for supply chain optimization, inventory management, and quality control in manufacturing.

Early IoT applications extended beyond healthcare, transportation, and smart homes. For instance, agricultural IoT systems employed sensors to monitor soil moisture, temperature, and crop health, enabling farmers to optimize irrigation, fertilization, and pest control. Environmental monitoring systems utilized IoT technologies to gather data on air quality, water pollution, and weather conditions, aiding in environmental conservation efforts and urban planning.

Moreover, smart cities emerged as a visionary concept driven by IoT. Cities implemented IoT technologies to optimize resource management, improve traffic flow, enhance public safety, and provide better services to residents. IoT-based sensors and intelligent systems facilitated efficient waste management, parking management, and energy consumption monitoring, transforming cities into connected ecosystems that enhance livability and sustainability.

These early IoT applications represent a glimpse into the transformative power of interconnected devices and systems. By leveraging IoT technologies, industries and individuals gained the ability to collect and analyze vast amounts of data, automate processes, and make data-driven decisions. These pioneering examples laid the foundation for the widespread adoption and continuous evolution of IoT, as organizations and innovators continue to push the boundaries of what is possible in the interconnected world.

CHAPTER III
Core Components of IoT

A. Sensors and Actuators

Types of Sensors and Their Functionalities

Sensors are fundamental components of the Internet of Things (IoT) that enable devices to perceive and gather data from their surroundings. A wide range of sensors exists, each designed to capture specific types of information. Here are some common types of sensors used in IoT applications and their functionalities:

a) Temperature Sensors: These sensors measure ambient temperature and are vital in applications where temperature control is critical, such as climate control systems in smart homes or temperature monitoring in cold chain logistics.

b) Proximity Sensors: Proximity sensors detect the presence or absence of objects within a specific range. They are often used in automated systems for object detection, motion sensing, and touchless interfaces, such as automatic doors, occupancy detection, or touchless switches.

c) Pressure Sensors: Pressure sensors measure changes in pressure and are commonly used in industrial applications for monitoring fluid levels, air pressure, and hydraulic systems. They find applications in areas like smart agriculture for monitoring irrigation levels or in healthcare for monitoring blood pressure.

d) Accelerometers: Accelerometers measure acceleration or changes in motion. They are found in various devices, including fitness trackers, smartphones, and automotive systems. Accelerometers enable applications such as step counting, gesture recognition, and vehicle stability control.

e) Light Sensors: Light sensors, also known as ambient light sensors or photodetectors, measure light intensity. They are commonly used in automatic lighting systems, display brightness adjustment, and smart city applications like intelligent street lighting.

f) Humidity Sensors: Humidity sensors measure the moisture content in the air or other substances. They are employed in applications such as weather monitoring, indoor climate control, and agricultural systems for maintaining optimal humidity levels.

Role of Actuators in IoT Systems

While sensors gather data from the environment, actuators allow IoT systems to interact with and influence the physical world. Actuators are devices that convert electrical signals into mechanical motion or perform specific actions based on the instructions received. They are essential for translating the digital information collected by sensors into physical responses. Here are some examples of actuators and their roles in IoT systems:

a) Motors: Motors are commonly used actuators that generate rotational or linear motion. They play a crucial role in applications such as robotics, industrial automation, and smart home devices like automated curtains or door locks.

b) Valves: Valves control the flow of fluids or gases. In IoT applications, valves are employed in water management systems, irrigation systems, or industrial processes that require precise fluid control.

c) Servo Motors: Servo motors are specialized motors that provide precise control of angular or rotational positions. They are widely used in robotics, drones, and autonomous systems where accurate movement control is required.

d) Solenoids: Solenoids are electromechanical devices that convert electrical energy into linear motion. They are commonly used in applications like electronic door locks, automated door openers, and fluid control systems.

e) LED Lights: Light-emitting diodes (LEDs) are versatile actuators used in IoT systems for their ability to emit light in various colors. LEDs find applications in smart lighting systems, visual notifications, and status indicators.

Actuators are integral components that enable IoT devices to respond to the data collected by sensors, allowing them to interact with the physical world. By combining sensors and actuators, IoT systems can gather information from the environment, process it, and initiate actions based on the analyzed data. This seamless integration of sensing and actuation capabilities forms the foundation of IoT's transformative potential in various domains, ranging from smart homes and industrial automation to healthcare and environmental monitoring.

B. Connectivity

Wireless Communication Protocols

Connectivity is a critical component of the Internet of Things (IoT) ecosystem, enabling devices to communicate and exchange data seamlessly. Wireless communication protocols play a vital role in establishing reliable and efficient connections between IoT devices. Here are some commonly used wireless communication protocols in IoT:

a) Wi-Fi: Wi-Fi, based on the IEEE 802.11 standard, is a widely adopted wireless communication protocol that enables high-speed data transmission over short distances. Wi-Fi offers robust connectivity and is commonly used in smart homes, offices, and public spaces, where devices require internet access and high bandwidth.

b) Bluetooth: Bluetooth technology is ideal for short-range communication between devices. It is commonly used for connecting IoT devices in close proximity, such as wireless headphones, smartwatches, and home automation systems. Bluetooth Low Energy (BLE) is a power-efficient variant of Bluetooth designed for IoT applications that require low energy consumption.

c) Zigbee: Zigbee is a low-power wireless communication protocol that facilitates communication between IoT devices over short to medium distances. It is commonly used in home automation, industrial automation, and smart lighting systems. Zigbee's low power consumption and mesh network topology make it suitable for applications that require long battery life and reliable communication.

d) Z-Wave: Z-Wave is a wireless communication protocol designed for smart home applications. It operates in the sub-GHz frequency range and offers low power consumption and extended range. Z-Wave is known for its interoperability, enabling devices from different manufacturers to communicate and work together seamlessly.

e) Cellular Networks: Cellular networks, such as 4G LTE and upcoming 5G, provide wide-area connectivity for IoT devices. Cellular connectivity is suitable for applications that require mobility or coverage in remote areas. It enables IoT devices to communicate with each other and the internet over long distances, making it valuable for applications like asset tracking, transportation, and smart cities.

Network Infrastructures Supporting IoT

In addition to wireless communication protocols, IoT relies on robust network infrastructures to support the connectivity requirements of interconnected devices. Here are two types of network infrastructures commonly used in IoT:

a) Local Area Network (LAN): A LAN refers to a network infrastructure that connects devices within a limited geographical area, such as a home, office, or industrial facility. LANs typically utilize wired or wireless connections to facilitate communication between IoT devices and gateways. LANs provide local connectivity and often serve as the foundation for smart home or industrial IoT deployments.

b) Wide Area Network (WAN): A WAN encompasses a broader geographical area and enables communication between devices that are geographically dispersed. The internet itself can be considered a global WAN that connects IoT devices worldwide. WAN connectivity allows IoT devices to transmit data over long distances and enables centralized control and monitoring of distributed IoT deployments.

To enable seamless communication and integration across different network infrastructures, IoT gateways play a crucial role. These gateways serve as intermediaries between IoT devices and the internet or cloud platforms, facilitating data transmission, protocol translation, and security enforcement.

Furthermore, cloud computing platforms and edge computing technologies enhance the capabilities of IoT networks by providing scalable storage, computational power, and real-time analytics. Cloud platforms enable the storage and processing of vast amounts of IoT data, while edge computing brings data processing closer to the source, reducing latency and enabling real-time decision-making.

In conclusion, connectivity is a core component of IoT, and wireless communication protocols are the backbone of device-to-device communication. The choice of wireless protocols depends on factors such as range, power consumption, bandwidth requirements, and deployment scenarios. Additionally, network infrastructures, including LANs and WANs, support the connectivity needs of IoT devices, enabling seamless data transmission and integration. Together, these components lay the foundation for the interconnectedness and data exchange that drive the transformative potential of IoT in various domains.

C. Data Management and Analytics

Data Collection and Storage in IoT

Data collection is a crucial aspect of the Internet of Things (IoT), as it involves gathering and organizing data from various connected devices and sensors. In IoT systems, a massive amount of data is generated, and effective data collection strategies are necessary to ensure its reliability and usability. Here are some key considerations for data collection and storage in IoT:

a) Sensors and Devices: IoT devices equipped with sensors play a vital role in data collection. These sensors capture information from the physical world, such as temperature, humidity, motion, and more. IoT devices communicate with each other and transmit the collected data to centralized systems for storage and analysis.

b) Data Sampling: In IoT, data sampling refers to the process of selecting and capturing data points at specific intervals. The frequency of data sampling depends on the requirements of the application and the desired level of granularity. For example, sensors in environmental monitoring systems may collect data every few seconds, while sensors in a smart home may collect data every few minutes.

c) Edge Data Processing: Edge computing has emerged as a valuable approach in IoT data management. Edge devices, such as gateways or edge servers, perform data processing and filtering at the network edge, closer to the data source. This reduces latency, conserves bandwidth, and allows for real-time decision-making. Edge processing helps filter out irrelevant or redundant data before transmitting it to the cloud or centralized servers.

d) Data Protocols and Standards: Standardization of data protocols is essential for ensuring interoperability and efficient data collection in IoT systems. Protocols like MQTT (Message Queuing Telemetry Transport) and CoAP

(Constrained Application Protocol) facilitate lightweight and efficient data transfer between devices and the cloud.

e) Data Security and Privacy: Given the sensitive nature of IoT data, robust security measures are critical. Encryption, authentication, access control, and data anonymization techniques help protect data privacy and prevent unauthorized access. Implementing security measures at the device level, network level, and data storage level is crucial to safeguard IoT data.

Regarding data storage, IoT systems deal with vast amounts of data generated by numerous interconnected devices. To effectively manage this data, various storage solutions can be utilized, including:

a) Cloud Storage: Cloud computing platforms offer scalable and reliable storage for IoT data. Cloud storage allows organizations to store and access data in a centralized manner, providing flexibility, scalability, and ease of management. Cloud storage also enables efficient data sharing and collaboration among different stakeholders.

b) Distributed Storage: Distributed storage systems, such as distributed file systems and NoSQL databases, provide the capability to store and process data across multiple nodes. These systems ensure data redundancy, fault tolerance, and high availability. Distributed storage is well-suited for IoT deployments that require resilience and fault-tolerant data storage.

c) Edge Storage: Edge computing architectures also incorporate edge storage, where data is stored and processed locally on edge devices. Edge storage reduces latency, improves real-time responsiveness, and allows for efficient local data processing. This approach is beneficial in scenarios where immediate access to data is required, or when intermittent network connectivity may occur.

Data Analytics for Extracting Insights

Data analytics is a crucial component of IoT, enabling organizations to derive valuable insights and actionable intelligence from the vast amounts of collected data. Here are some key aspects of data analytics in IoT:

a) Real-Time Analytics: IoT generates a continuous stream of real-time data. Real-time analytics techniques, such as stream processing and complex event processing, enable the immediate analysis of data as it flows in, allowing organizations to respond swiftly to critical events or anomalies.

b) Data Preprocessing: Data preprocessing involves cleaning, transforming, and aggregating raw IoT data to improve its quality and relevance. Preprocessing techniques, including data filtering, normalization, and outlier detection, help remove noise, inconsistencies, or irrelevant data points, ensuring accurate and reliable analytics results.

c) Descriptive, Predictive, and Prescriptive Analytics: Descriptive analytics focuses on summarizing historical data to understand past events and trends. Predictive analytics utilizes statistical modeling and machine learning algorithms to forecast future outcomes and detect patterns. Prescriptive analytics takes the analysis a step further by suggesting optimal actions based on the insights gained from the data.

d) Machine Learning and AI: Machine learning algorithms and artificial intelligence techniques are employed in IoT analytics to uncover hidden patterns, detect anomalies, and make predictions. These techniques enable intelligent decision-making, predictive maintenance, anomaly detection, and personalized user experiences.

e) Data Visualization: Presenting analytics results in a visually appealing and intuitive manner is crucial for effective communication and decision-making. Data visualization techniques, including charts, graphs, and dashboards, help stakeholders understand complex data patterns, trends, and correlations quickly.

Data management and analytics in IoT systems are essential for unlocking the full potential of collected data. Effective data collection strategies, combined with robust storage solutions, facilitate reliable and scalable data management. By leveraging advanced analytics techniques, organizations can gain valuable insights, improve operational efficiency, and drive innovation in various sectors, ranging from healthcare and manufacturing to smart cities and environmental monitoring.

CHAPTER IV
Applications of IoT

A. Smart Homes and Home Automation

IoT Devices for Home Security

The emergence of the Internet of Things (IoT) has revolutionized the concept of home security, making it smarter, more accessible, and more efficient. IoT devices have introduced a new era of interconnectedness and automation, enhancing home security measures. Here are two key aspects of IoT in home security:

a) Smart Cameras and Video Doorbells: IoT-enabled cameras and video doorbells provide enhanced security by allowing homeowners to monitor their premises remotely. These devices offer real-time video streaming and two-way communication, enabling users to see and interact with visitors, even when they are away from home. Motion detection and intelligent algorithms help identify potential threats or suspicious activities, triggering alerts and notifications on users' smartphones. Cloud storage enables the storage of recorded footage, providing valuable evidence in the event of security incidents.

b) Smart Locks and Alarm Systems: IoT-based smart locks and alarm systems enhance home security by offering convenient access control and real-time monitoring. Smart locks allow homeowners to remotely lock and unlock doors, eliminating the need for physical keys. Integration with mobile apps and voice assistants enables seamless control and monitoring. IoT-based alarm systems use sensors to detect unauthorized entry or suspicious activities, triggering alerts and activating sirens or notifications. Homeowners can receive instant notifications and take appropriate actions, ensuring the safety of their homes and possessions.

These IoT devices provide homeowners with increased control, flexibility, and peace of mind when it comes to home security. By leveraging connectivity and intelligent algorithms, IoT-based home security systems offer proactive protection and real-time monitoring, reducing the risk of break-ins and providing an added layer of security for residents.

IoT technologies play a significant role in energy management and efficiency in smart homes. By connecting various devices and systems, IoT enables intelligent control and optimization of energy consumption. Here are two key aspects of IoT in energy management and efficiency:

a) Smart Thermostats: IoT-enabled smart thermostats provide precise control over heating, ventilation, and air conditioning (HVAC) systems, optimizing energy usage. These thermostats learn and adapt to homeowners' preferences and behavior, automatically adjusting temperature settings based on occupancy, time of day, and weather conditions. Remote access via mobile apps allows users to monitor and control their HVAC systems from anywhere, ensuring energy efficiency and cost savings.

b) Energy Monitoring and Analytics: IoT-based energy monitoring systems utilize smart meters and energy sensors to track and analyze energy consumption patterns in real-time. These systems provide homeowners with detailed insights into their energy usage, helping identify energy-hungry appliances, peak consumption periods, and areas for potential energy savings. By visualizing energy data through user-friendly dashboards, homeowners can make informed decisions about energy usage, implement energy-efficient practices, and reduce their carbon footprint.

IoT-driven energy management empowers homeowners to actively participate in sustainable practices and reduce their energy consumption. By optimizing energy usage, smart homes contribute to energy efficiency, cost savings, and environmental sustainability.

In summary, IoT applications in smart homes and home automation have transformed the way we approach home security and energy management. IoT devices such as smart cameras, video doorbells, smart locks, and alarm systems offer enhanced security measures, enabling remote monitoring, access control, and real-time alerts. In energy management, IoT facilitates intelligent control of HVAC systems through smart thermostats and provides energy monitoring and analytics tools to optimize energy consumption. As smart homes continue to evolve, IoT-driven innovations ensure safer, more energy-efficient, and convenient living environments for homeowners.

B. Industrial IoT (IIoT)

Automation and Optimization in Manufacturing

The Industrial Internet of Things (IIoT) has revolutionized the manufacturing industry by driving automation, enhancing productivity, and optimizing operations. IIoT leverages interconnected devices, sensors, and data analytics to transform traditional factories into smart and efficient production environments. Here are two key aspects of IIoT in manufacturing:

a) Automation: IIoT enables a higher degree of automation in manufacturing processes. Connected sensors and devices gather real-time data on various parameters such as temperature, pressure, and machine performance. This data is transmitted to centralized systems for analysis and control, enabling real-time monitoring and automation of production lines. Automated processes minimize human intervention, reduce errors, improve quality, and increase production throughput.

b) Optimization: IIoT facilitates the optimization of manufacturing operations by providing valuable insights and actionable intelligence. Advanced analytics techniques applied to the collected data enable the identification of bottlenecks, inefficiencies, and areas for improvement. Manufacturers can leverage these insights to optimize production scheduling, inventory management, resource allocation, and energy consumption. Optimization based on real-time data helps streamline operations, reduce costs, and improve overall efficiency.

IIoT enables the concept of "smart factories" where interconnected devices, machines, and systems work together in a synchronized manner, enabling real-time decision-making and adaptive manufacturing processes. By embracing automation and optimization through IIoT, manufacturers gain a competitive edge by achieving higher productivity, cost savings, and improved product quality.

Predictive Maintenance and Asset Tracking

Predictive maintenance and asset tracking are key applications of IIoT that have transformed maintenance practices in the manufacturing industry. IIoT systems enable the continuous monitoring of equipment and assets, facilitating proactive maintenance and reducing downtime. Here are two important aspects of IIoT in predictive maintenance and asset tracking:

a) Predictive Maintenance: Traditional maintenance practices are often reactive, relying on scheduled maintenance or fixing issues after equipment failure. IIoT, on the other hand, allows for predictive maintenance. Sensors embedded in machines and equipment collect data on variables like temperature, vibration, and performance parameters. This data is analyzed using machine learning and predictive algorithms to identify patterns and indicators of potential failures. By predicting maintenance needs in advance, manufacturers can schedule maintenance activities, order spare parts, and prevent unplanned downtime, leading to significant cost savings and increased equipment availability.

b) Asset Tracking: IIoT enables accurate and real-time tracking of assets throughout the manufacturing facility or supply chain. IoT-enabled asset tracking systems utilize technologies such as RFID tags, GPS, or Bluetooth beacons to monitor the location, movement, and condition of assets. This helps manufacturers optimize asset utilization, improve inventory management, prevent loss or theft, and enhance supply chain visibility. Asset tracking in IIoT enhances efficiency, reduces manual effort, and enables better asset lifecycle management.

The combination of predictive maintenance and asset tracking in IIoT transforms maintenance strategies from reactive to proactive, minimizing equipment downtime, reducing costs, and optimizing resource allocation. Manufacturers can achieve higher equipment reliability, extend asset lifespan, and ensure smooth operations by leveraging IIoT technologies.

In conclusion, IIoT plays a transformative role in the manufacturing industry. Automation and optimization enabled by IIoT enhance productivity and efficiency in production processes. Predictive maintenance and asset tracking in IIoT facilitate proactive maintenance strategies, reducing downtime and improving equipment reliability. By embracing IIoT, manufacturers gain a competitive advantage by streamlining operations, increasing productivity, reducing costs, and ensuring the seamless functioning of smart factories in the digital era.

C. Smart Cities

Urban Infrastructure Management

The concept of smart cities harnesses the power of the Internet of Things (IoT) to improve the efficiency, sustainability, and livability of urban areas. IoT technologies enable the monitoring, management, and optimization of various aspects of urban infrastructure.

Here are two key applications of IoT in urban infrastructure management:

a) Smart Energy Grids: IoT plays a crucial role in the creation of smart energy grids, which optimize energy generation, distribution, and consumption in cities. IoT sensors, smart meters, and data analytics enable real-time monitoring of energy usage, peak demand periods, and grid performance. This information helps utility companies manage energy supply, balance the grid, and implement demand-response strategies. Smart grids enhance energy efficiency, reduce wastage, and promote the integration of renewable energy sources, contributing to a more sustainable and resilient urban energy infrastructure.

b) Waste Management: IoT-based waste management systems revolutionize the collection and disposal of waste in cities. Smart bins equipped with sensors and fill-level indicators transmit data to waste management authorities, enabling optimized waste collection routes and schedules. Real-time monitoring helps prevent overflowing bins, reduces unnecessary collection trips, and minimizes the environmental impact of waste management operations. Additionally, IoT-enabled waste sorting and recycling systems improve the efficiency of recycling processes, promoting sustainable waste management practices in smart cities.

By leveraging IoT in urban infrastructure management, smart cities can achieve greater resource efficiency, reduced environmental impact, and improved quality of life for residents.

Traffic and Transportation Solutions

IoT offers innovative solutions for optimizing traffic flow, improving transportation systems, and enhancing the overall mobility experience in smart cities. Here are two key aspects of IoT in traffic and transportation solutions:

a) Intelligent Traffic Management: IoT enables intelligent traffic management systems that monitor traffic conditions in real-time. Connected sensors, cameras, and smart traffic lights gather data on traffic density, congestion, and road conditions. This information is analyzed to optimize traffic signal timing, dynamically adjust lane configurations, and provide real-time traffic updates to drivers. Smart traffic management systems help reduce congestion, improve traffic flow, and enhance road safety in urban areas.

b) Smart Parking: IoT-based smart parking systems offer real-time information on parking availability, guiding drivers to vacant parking spaces and reducing the time spent searching for parking. IoT sensors installed in parking lots or on-street parking spaces detect occupancy and transmit data to mobile apps or digital signage. Drivers can access this information to find the nearest available parking spot, reducing traffic congestion, carbon emissions, and frustration associated with parking difficulties.

IoT-enabled traffic and transportation solutions in smart cities enhance mobility, reduce travel times, and promote sustainable transportation options. By optimizing traffic flow and improving parking management, smart cities enhance the overall urban transportation experience for residents and visitors.

In conclusion, IoT applications in smart cities revolutionize urban infrastructure management and transportation systems. Smart energy grids optimize energy usage and promote sustainability. IoT-based waste management systems enhance efficiency and environmental sustainability in waste disposal. Intelligent traffic management and smart parking solutions improve traffic flow, reduce congestion, and enhance mobility. By embracing IoT, smart cities leverage technology to create more efficient, sustainable, and livable urban environments for their residents.

D. Healthcare and Wearable Devices

Remote Patient Monitoring

The Internet of Things (IoT) has transformed healthcare by enabling remote patient monitoring, empowering individuals to take control of their health and improving healthcare outcomes. IoT-based wearable devices and remote monitoring systems offer real-time health data collection, analysis, and communication between patients and healthcare providers. Here are two key aspects of IoT in remote patient monitoring:

a) Vital Signs Monitoring: Wearable devices equipped with sensors, such as smartwatches or fitness trackers, monitor vital signs like heart rate, blood pressure, and sleep patterns. These devices continuously collect and transmit data to healthcare providers, allowing for remote monitoring of patients' health conditions. Remote vital signs monitoring enables early detection of abnormalities, supports chronic disease management, and enhances preventive care strategies.

b) Chronic Disease Management: IoT-based remote monitoring systems play a crucial role in managing chronic conditions like diabetes, hypertension, or respiratory diseases. Connected devices, such as glucose monitors or inhalers, transmit data to healthcare providers, who can remotely track patients' health parameters, medication adherence, and symptoms. This allows for timely intervention, adjustment of treatment plans, and personalized care, reducing hospital admissions, improving patient outcomes, and enhancing quality of life.

Remote patient monitoring in healthcare brings several benefits, including reduced healthcare costs, improved patient engagement, and enhanced access to care. Patients can stay connected with their healthcare providers, receive personalized guidance, and actively participate in their own well-being.

Fitness Tracking and Personalized Healthcare

IoT-enabled wearable devices have revolutionized fitness tracking and personalized healthcare, empowering individuals to monitor their physical activity, track their health goals, and receive personalized insights. Here are two key aspects of IoT in fitness tracking and personalized healthcare:

a) Activity Tracking: Wearable fitness trackers equipped with sensors monitor various physical activities, including steps taken, distance traveled, calories burned, and exercise intensity. These devices provide real-time feedback, motivate individuals to maintain an active lifestyle, and set fitness goals. Connected to mobile apps or online platforms, fitness trackers enable users to track their progress, analyze trends, and receive personalized recommendations for a healthier lifestyle.

b) Personalized Health Insights: IoT devices and platforms collect and analyze health data, generating personalized insights for individuals. Advanced analytics algorithms process data from multiple sources, such as fitness trackers, sleep monitors, and dietary trackers, to provide personalized health recommendations. These insights can include exercise recommendations, sleep optimization strategies, stress management techniques, and nutritional advice. Personalized healthcare insights empower individuals to make informed decisions about their well-being and take proactive steps towards better health outcomes.

By leveraging IoT in fitness tracking and personalized healthcare, individuals gain greater awareness of their health, receive personalized guidance, and take active control of their well-being. This promotes a preventive approach to healthcare, leading to better health outcomes and improved quality of life.

In conclusion, IoT applications in healthcare and wearable devices have revolutionized remote patient monitoring, fitness tracking, and personalized healthcare. Remote patient monitoring allows for continuous health data collection and remote communication with healthcare providers, supporting chronic disease management and preventive care. Fitness tracking and personalized healthcare empower individuals to monitor their physical activity, set health goals, and receive personalized insights for a healthier lifestyle. By embracing IoT in healthcare, individuals can actively participate in their own well-being, leading to improved health outcomes, enhanced patient engagement, and a more proactive approach to healthcare.

CHAPTER V
Challenges and Considerations in IoT

A. Security and Privacy

Threats and Vulnerabilities in IoT Systems

The rapid proliferation of the Internet of Things (IoT) brings with it significant security and privacy challenges. As more devices become interconnected, the attack surface for potential threats expands, making it essential to understand and address the vulnerabilities present in IoT systems. Here are some common threats and vulnerabilities associated with IoT:

a) Device Vulnerabilities: IoT devices often have limited computing power and memory, making them susceptible to attacks. Weak default passwords, unpatched firmware, and inadequate security controls can make IoT devices vulnerable to unauthorized access, hijacking, or compromise.

b) Data Breaches: IoT systems collect and transmit vast amounts of sensitive data, including personal information and behavioral patterns. Inadequate encryption, insecure data storage, or unsecured data transmission can lead to data breaches, compromising user privacy and exposing sensitive information to unauthorized parties.

c) Denial of Service (DoS) Attacks: IoT devices connected to the internet can be targeted in distributed denial of service (DDoS) attacks. Attackers flood the network or devices with a massive volume of requests, overwhelming the resources and rendering them unavailable. These attacks disrupt normal operations and can impact critical infrastructure systems.

d) Malware and Botnets: IoT devices can be infected with malware and incorporated into botnets, turning them into a network of compromised devices under the control of an attacker. Botnets can be utilized for various malicious activities, including launching DDoS attacks, spreading malware, or stealing sensitive information.

e) Lack of Standardization: The lack of standardized security practices and protocols across IoT devices and platforms can create vulnerabilities. Inconsistent implementation of security measures, fragmented ecosystems, and interoperability issues make it challenging to ensure robust security across diverse IoT deployments.

Strategies for Securing IoT Devices and Data

Securing IoT devices and data requires a multi-layered approach that addresses vulnerabilities at different levels. Here are some strategies for enhancing the security of IoT devices and data:

a) Strong Authentication and Access Controls: Implementing strong authentication mechanisms, such as unique device credentials and multi-factor authentication, helps prevent unauthorized access to IoT devices and systems. Additionally, access controls based on user roles and privileges limit the actions that can be performed by different users or devices within the IoT ecosystem.

b) Robust Encryption: Encryption techniques, such as Transport Layer Security (TLS) and Advanced Encryption Standard (AES), should be employed to secure data both in transit and at rest. End-to-end encryption ensures that data remains encrypted throughout its journey from IoT devices to the cloud or other destinations.

c) Regular Firmware Updates and Patch Management: Manufacturers should provide regular firmware updates to address security vulnerabilities and patch known issues. IoT devices should support over-the-air (OTA) updates, making it easier to distribute patches and security fixes promptly.

d) Network Segmentation: Segregating IoT devices into separate network segments limits the impact of potential breaches. By isolating IoT devices from critical systems and implementing proper network segmentation, the potential for lateral movement within the network can be minimized.

e) Continuous Monitoring and Intrusion Detection: Implementing robust monitoring systems helps detect anomalous behavior, intrusion attempts, or unauthorized access to IoT devices. Intrusion detection systems (IDS) and security analytics platforms can analyze network traffic and device behavior patterns to identify potential threats in real-time.

f) Privacy by Design: Privacy considerations should be incorporated into the design and development of IoT systems. Adopting privacy-enhancing technologies, such as data anonymization or differential privacy techniques, helps protect user privacy while still enabling data analysis for valuable insights.

g) Collaboration and Standardization: Industry collaboration and the establishment of standards and best practices are essential for ensuring a secure IoT ecosystem. Sharing knowledge, threat intelligence, and security guidelines among manufacturers, service providers, and regulatory bodies helps create a more secure environment for IoT deployments.

Securing IoT devices and data is an ongoing effort that requires a proactive and collaborative approach. By implementing robust security measures, staying vigilant against emerging threats, and fostering industry-wide collaboration, the potential risks associated with IoT can be mitigated, ensuring a safer and more secure IoT landscape.

In conclusion, security and privacy are critical considerations in the IoT landscape. Understanding and addressing threats and vulnerabilities is crucial to safeguarding IoT devices and data. By implementing strategies such as strong authentication, encryption, regular updates, network segmentation, and continuous monitoring, the security posture of IoT systems can be significantly enhanced. Collaboration, standardization, and privacy-focused design practices further contribute to the overall security and privacy of the IoT ecosystem.

B. Interoperability and Standardization

Ensuring Compatibility Among Different IoT Devices

One of the key challenges in the Internet of Things (IoT) is achieving interoperability and ensuring compatibility among different IoT devices. With the proliferation of diverse IoT devices from various manufacturers, it becomes crucial to establish seamless communication and data exchange between them. Here are some considerations for ensuring compatibility in the IoT ecosystem:

a) Data Formats and Protocols: IoT devices may use different data formats and communication protocols, making it challenging to exchange data effectively. Standardizing data formats and adopting interoperable protocols, such as MQTT (Message Queuing Telemetry Transport) or CoAP (Constrained Application Protocol), promotes compatibility and facilitates seamless integration between devices.

b) Connectivity and Network Compatibility: IoT devices often utilize different connectivity technologies, such as Wi-Fi, Bluetooth, Zigbee, or cellular networks. Ensuring compatibility across different network protocols and connectivity options is essential for enabling interoperability among devices. Additionally, compatibility with existing network infrastructure and protocols allows for easier integration of IoT devices into established systems.

c) Device Discovery and Plug-and-Play Integration: Simplifying the process of device discovery and enabling plug-and-play integration promotes compatibility among IoT devices. Universal device discovery protocols, such as Universal Plug and Play (UPnP) or Zero Configuration Networking (Zeroconf), facilitate automatic device recognition and configuration, minimizing the effort required for device setup and interoperability.

d) Application Programming Interfaces (APIs): Well-defined and standardized APIs enable interoperability by providing a common interface for communication and data exchange between IoT devices and applications. Open APIs and industry standards encourage developers to build applications that can interact with diverse IoT devices seamlessly.

e) Semantic Interoperability: Semantic interoperability ensures that devices can understand and interpret data from different sources. Common data models and ontologies enable meaningful communication and data exchange, allowing devices to share information accurately and perform desired actions based on shared understanding.

Importance of Industry Standards in IoT

Industry standards play a crucial role in the successful adoption and widespread deployment of IoT solutions. Standardization efforts contribute to interoperability, reliability, security, and scalability of IoT ecosystems. Here are some reasons why industry standards are important in IoT:

a) Interoperability: Standards enable different IoT devices, systems, and platforms to work together seamlessly. They ensure compatibility, enabling devices from various manufacturers to communicate, exchange data, and operate within a common framework. Interoperability reduces complexity, fosters innovation, and expands the possibilities for developing integrated IoT solutions.

b) Reliability and Quality Assurance: Standards provide guidelines and specifications that ensure a certain level of reliability and quality in IoT devices and systems. Compliance with standards helps manufacturers deliver products that meet established criteria, ensuring better performance, reliability, and interoperability for end-users.

c) Security: Industry standards contribute to the security of IoT systems by defining best practices, protocols, and mechanisms to protect devices, data, and communication. Standards address security considerations such as authentication, encryption, access control, and secure firmware updates. Compliance with security standards helps mitigate vulnerabilities and build more robust and secure IoT deployments.

d) Scalability and Future-Proofing: Standards enable scalability by ensuring that IoT solutions can grow and evolve without significant disruptions. They provide a foundation for interoperability and compatibility as new devices and technologies emerge. Adherence to industry standards future-proofs IoT deployments, allowing for seamless integration of new devices, services, and applications.

e) Market Adoption and Ecosystem Development: Standards encourage broader market adoption of IoT solutions by establishing a common language and framework. They promote a level playing field, enabling vendors and developers to focus on innovation and value-added services rather than reinventing basic functionality. Standards foster collaboration, stimulate competition, and drive the growth of the IoT ecosystem as a whole.

In conclusion, ensuring compatibility and interoperability among different IoT devices is crucial for the success and scalability of IoT deployments. Industry standards play a vital role in achieving this interoperability, promoting reliability, security, and scalability in IoT ecosystems. By adopting standardized data formats, communication protocols, APIs, and network compatibility, the IoT industry can overcome compatibility challenges and drive innovation, ensuring seamless integration and enhanced functionality across diverse IoT devices and systems.

C. Ethical and Social Implications

Privacy Concerns and Data Ownership

The widespread adoption of the Internet of Things (IoT) raises significant ethical and social implications, particularly regarding privacy concerns and data ownership. As IoT devices collect vast amounts of personal data, questions arise about how this data is used, who has access to it, and the implications for individuals' privacy. Here are some key considerations related to privacy and data ownership in the context of IoT:

a) Data Privacy: IoT devices gather data from various sources, including sensors, cameras, and user interactions. The collection, storage, and processing of this data raise privacy concerns as it can contain sensitive personal information. Ensuring transparent data collection practices, obtaining user consent, and implementing robust data protection mechanisms, such as encryption and anonymization, are essential for safeguarding individuals' privacy.

b) Consent and Control: Users should have control over their data and be informed about how it is collected, used, and shared. Clear consent mechanisms, allowing users to make informed choices, should be in place. Users should also have the ability to modify or revoke their consent and have control over the granularity of data sharing preferences.

c) Data Ownership: The ownership of IoT-generated data is a complex issue. Data generated by IoT devices may involve personal, environmental, or communal information. Determining ownership rights and establishing frameworks for fair data sharing and access are necessary to address the ethical and legal implications of data ownership in the IoT ecosystem.

d) Data Security: Ensuring robust data security measures is crucial to protect personal information from unauthorized access, breaches, or misuse. Encryption, access controls, and secure communication protocols are essential to safeguard IoT data from potential security threats.

The advent of IoT technologies has a profound impact on employment and society, presenting both opportunities and challenges. Here are some key considerations regarding the impact of IoT:

a) Job Displacement: IoT-driven automation and advancements in artificial intelligence may lead to job displacement and changes in the labor market. Tasks that can be automated through IoT technologies may replace certain roles, potentially resulting in job losses or shifts in job requirements. However, new job opportunities may also arise in areas such as IoT development, data analytics, and cybersecurity.

b) Workforce Skills and Training: The widespread adoption of IoT necessitates a skilled workforce capable of developing, deploying, and maintaining IoT systems. It is crucial to provide training and education to equip individuals with the necessary skills to adapt to changing job requirements and take advantage of emerging opportunities in the IoT ecosystem.

c) Social Inequality: The digital divide and access to IoT technologies can exacerbate existing social inequalities. Unequal access to IoT infrastructure, connectivity, and digital literacy can result in disparities in benefits derived from IoT advancements. It is important to address these disparities and ensure equitable access to IoT technologies, bridging the digital divide and promoting inclusivity.

d) Ethical and Social Implications: IoT raises ethical considerations, such as the ethical use of data, algorithmic biases, and the potential for surveillance. Ensuring transparency, fairness, and accountability in the design, development, and deployment of IoT systems is essential to mitigate potential ethical risks and societal harms.

e) Societal Benefits: IoT technologies have the potential to bring significant societal benefits, such as improved healthcare, enhanced resource efficiency, and safer cities. By leveraging IoT to address societal challenges, such as environmental sustainability or public safety, we can create positive social impact and improve the overall well-being of communities.

As IoT technologies continue to evolve, it is crucial to address the ethical and social implications associated with privacy concerns, data ownership, employment, and societal impacts. Engaging in open dialogue, establishing ethical frameworks, and implementing policies that prioritize privacy, fairness, and inclusivity can ensure that IoT advancements contribute to a more sustainable, equitable, and beneficial future for society.

CHAPTER VI
Future Trends and Possibilities

A. Artificial Intelligence (AI) and Machine Learning in IoT

Artificial Intelligence (AI) and machine learning have emerged as powerful technologies with the potential to transform the Internet of Things (IoT) landscape. As IoT continues to evolve, AI and machine learning play a crucial role in enhancing the capabilities and expanding the possibilities of IoT systems. Here are some future trends and possibilities for AI and machine learning in IoT:

- ❖ Advanced Data Analytics: AI and machine learning algorithms enable sophisticated data analytics in IoT systems. By leveraging AI techniques, IoT devices can process and analyze large volumes of data in real-time, identifying patterns, anomalies, and valuable insights. Advanced analytics facilitate predictive and prescriptive analytics, enabling proactive decision-making, anomaly detection, and real-time optimization of IoT processes.

❖ Predictive Maintenance and Anomaly Detection: AI and machine learning enable predictive maintenance in IoT deployments. By analyzing historical data and real-time sensor inputs, AI algorithms can predict equipment failures, schedule maintenance activities, and optimize maintenance processes. Machine learning models can detect anomalies in sensor data, alerting operators to potential issues or deviations from normal behavior, enabling timely interventions and reducing downtime.

❖ Intelligent Edge Computing: Edge computing, combined with AI and machine learning, empowers IoT devices to perform complex computations and decision-making at the edge of the network. This reduces latency, enhances real-time responsiveness, and optimizes bandwidth utilization. AI algorithms running at the edge can analyze data locally, make intelligent decisions, and transmit only relevant information to the cloud, reducing data transfer and processing costs.

❖ Autonomous IoT Systems: AI and machine learning algorithms enable IoT systems to operate autonomously and adapt to changing conditions. Autonomous IoT systems can learn from data, make intelligent decisions, and take actions without human intervention. For example, self-driving vehicles, smart grids, and intelligent home automation systems can leverage AI and machine learning to operate efficiently, optimize energy usage, and provide personalized experiences.

❖ Enhanced Security and Anomaly Detection: AI and machine learning can strengthen IoT security by identifying potential threats and detecting anomalies in real-time. Machine learning models can learn from patterns of normal behavior and detect deviations that indicate potential security breaches or malicious activities. AI-powered security solutions can continuously learn and adapt to evolving threats, providing proactive defense mechanisms against cyber-attacks in IoT systems.

❖ Personalized and Context-Aware Experiences: AI and machine learning enable IoT systems to provide personalized and context-aware experiences to users. By analyzing user preferences, behavior patterns, and contextual information, IoT devices can adapt their functionality, tailor recommendations, and deliver personalized services. This enhances user satisfaction, improves efficiency, and creates more meaningful interactions with IoT systems.

❖ Intelligent Energy Management: AI and machine learning techniques can optimize energy management in IoT deployments. By analyzing energy consumption patterns, environmental data, and user behavior, AI algorithms can make intelligent decisions to optimize energy usage, reduce wastage, and enhance energy efficiency in smart homes, buildings, and cities.

As AI and machine learning continue to advance, they will further revolutionize the capabilities of IoT systems, enabling autonomous decision-making, enhanced analytics, improved security, and personalized experiences. The convergence of AI and IoT opens up a world of possibilities, where intelligent, interconnected devices can learn, adapt, and optimize operations in various domains, creating smarter and more efficient environments for individuals and businesses.

B. Edge Computing and Fog Computing

Edge computing and fog computing are emerging paradigms that hold immense potential for the future of the Internet of Things (IoT). These computing models address the challenges of latency, bandwidth limitations, and privacy concerns associated with cloud-centric architectures. Here are some future trends and possibilities for edge computing and fog computing in IoT:

- ❖ Reduced Latency and Real-Time Responsiveness: Edge computing brings computation and data storage closer to the edge of the network, near IoT devices and sensors. By processing data locally at the edge, edge computing significantly reduces latency, enabling real-time responsiveness and faster decision-making. This is crucial for time-sensitive applications such as autonomous vehicles, industrial automation, and real-time monitoring systems.

❖ Bandwidth Optimization and Reduced Data Transfer: Edge computing and fog computing reduce the need to transfer large volumes of data to the cloud for processing and storage. Instead, data is processed locally at the edge or in fog nodes located in proximity to the devices. This optimized data transfer reduces bandwidth requirements, conserves network resources, and minimizes latency, making it suitable for IoT deployments with limited connectivity or high data volumes.

❖ Enhanced Privacy and Data Security: Edge computing enables data processing and analysis to occur locally on IoT devices or edge servers, reducing the need to send sensitive data to the cloud. This localization of data processing enhances privacy and data security, as critical information can be processed and analyzed within secure environments closer to the data source, minimizing the risk of data breaches and unauthorized access.

❖ Scalability and Decentralization: Edge computing and fog computing enable scalable IoT architectures by distributing computing resources across the network. Instead of relying solely on centralized cloud servers, edge devices and fog nodes contribute to the overall computing capacity. This decentralized approach enhances scalability, as IoT deployments can handle larger workloads and accommodate a growing number of connected devices.

❖ AI and Machine Learning at the Edge: Edge computing and fog computing can leverage AI and machine learning algorithms directly on IoT devices or at the edge of the network. This enables local AI-driven decision-making and real-time analytics without relying on cloud resources. By pushing intelligence to the edge, IoT systems can make autonomous decisions, optimize operations, and deliver personalized experiences, even in environments with limited connectivity.

❖ Hybrid Architectures: Fog computing complements edge computing by providing intermediate processing and storage capabilities between the edge and the cloud. Fog nodes, deployed in closer proximity to the edge devices, enable distributed computing, data caching, and analytics. This hybrid architecture leverages the strengths of edge computing and cloud computing, enabling a flexible and efficient IoT infrastructure.

❖ Support for Resource-Constrained Devices: Edge computing and fog computing are particularly beneficial for resource-constrained IoT devices that have limited processing power, memory, or battery life. By offloading computation to nearby edge servers or fog nodes, these devices can conserve energy, extend battery life, and perform tasks that would be challenging for them to handle independently.

As edge computing and fog computing technologies continue to advance, they will play a crucial role in enabling efficient, low-latency, and privacy-aware IoT systems. The convergence of edge computing, fog computing, and other technologies like AI and machine learning will unlock new possibilities for real-time analytics, intelligent decision-making, and distributed computing in diverse IoT applications.

C. 5G and Next-Generation Networks

The deployment of 5G networks and the development of next-generation network technologies are poised to revolutionize the Internet of Things (IoT) landscape, opening up exciting possibilities and paving the way for innovative applications. Here are some future trends and possibilities for 5G and next-generation networks in IoT:

* Enhanced Connectivity and Bandwidth: 5G networks offer significantly higher data transfer rates, lower latency, and improved network capacity compared to previous generations. This enhanced connectivity

enables seamless communication between a massive number of IoT devices, facilitating real-time data transmission and supporting applications that require high bandwidth, such as augmented reality (AR), virtual reality (VR), and immersive IoT experiences.

❖ Massive IoT Deployments: Next-generation networks, including 5G, are designed to support massive IoT deployments. These networks provide the capacity to connect billions of IoT devices simultaneously, creating a network infrastructure that can handle the demands of large-scale IoT applications across various sectors, including smart cities, industrial automation, and healthcare.

❖ Mission-Critical IoT Applications: 5G's low latency and high reliability make it suitable for mission-critical IoT applications that require real-time responsiveness and uninterrupted connectivity. Industries such as autonomous vehicles, remote surgery, and public safety can leverage 5G networks to enable ultra-responsive, reliable, and secure IoT systems that demand near-instantaneous communication and low-latency data transmission.

❖ Edge Computing at Scale: 5G networks enable distributed computing and edge computing at scale. With edge computing resources deployed closer to the network edge, near IoT devices, and 5G's low latency, processing data and running applications at the edge becomes more efficient. This facilitates real-time analytics, local decision-making, and reduced data transfer, enhancing the overall performance and responsiveness of IoT systems.

❖ Network Slicing and Service Differentiation: 5G networks introduce the concept of network slicing, allowing service providers to allocate specific portions of the network resources to different IoT applications or vertical industries. Network slicing enables customized network services tailored to the specific requirements of IoT applications, ensuring optimal performance, security, and reliability for diverse use cases.

❖ Enhanced Mobile Broadband (eMBB): 5G's enhanced mobile broadband capabilities provide faster and more reliable wireless connectivity, enabling seamless streaming of high-definition content, immersive experiences, and interactive applications. This opens up new possibilities for IoT applications in areas such as entertainment, gaming, and media.

❖ Low-Power IoT Devices: Next-generation networks, including 5G, are designed to support low-power IoT devices. Technologies such as Narrowband IoT (NB-IoT) and LTE-M enable efficient connectivity for battery-powered devices, extending their battery life and enabling long-range communication. This is particularly beneficial for applications such as smart agriculture, asset tracking, and environmental monitoring.

As 5G networks and next-generation network technologies continue to evolve and expand, they will unlock tremendous potential for IoT deployments. The combination of enhanced connectivity, massive IoT support, low latency, edge computing capabilities, and service differentiation will drive the development of innovative IoT applications across various industries. With 5G as the backbone, the IoT ecosystem will witness accelerated growth, increased efficiency, and the realization of futuristic IoT use cases that were previously unattainable.

D. Emerging Applications and Potential Disruptions

The future of the Internet of Things (IoT) holds vast potential for emerging applications that can transform industries, enhance efficiency, and improve the quality of life. As technology continues to advance, several exciting trends and disruptive possibilities are emerging. Here are some key areas of potential disruption and emerging applications in the IoT landscape:

❖ Smart Agriculture: IoT technologies are revolutionizing the agriculture sector by enabling precision farming, efficient resource management, and real-time monitoring. IoT sensors, drones, and satellite imagery help farmers optimize irrigation, monitor soil conditions, and detect crop diseases. Connected devices and data analytics enable data-driven decision-making, leading to increased crop yields, reduced resource wastage, and sustainable farming practices.

❖ Smart Retail and Supply Chain: IoT is transforming the retail industry by enabling seamless inventory management, personalized customer experiences, and efficient supply chain operations. RFID tags, IoT-enabled shelves, and sensors help retailers track inventory levels, monitor product freshness, and streamline logistics. IoT-powered analytics provide valuable insights into consumer behavior, enabling retailers to optimize operations, enhance customer engagement, and deliver personalized shopping experiences.

❖ Smart Energy Management: IoT plays a vital role in optimizing energy usage, improving grid efficiency, and promoting renewable energy integration. Smart energy meters, IoT-enabled home energy management systems, and grid monitoring devices allow for real-time energy consumption analysis, demand-response programs, and dynamic pricing. IoT sensors help optimize energy distribution, enhance grid stability, and facilitate the integration of distributed energy resources, such as solar panels and electric vehicles.

❖ Healthcare and Telemedicine: IoT is revolutionizing healthcare by enabling remote patient monitoring, personalized medicine, and telemedicine services. IoT devices, wearables, and connected healthcare systems enable continuous health monitoring, remote diagnostics, and proactive healthcare interventions. Real-time data collection and analytics support preventive care, early disease detection, and personalized treatment plans, leading to improved patient outcomes and cost savings.

❖ Smart Cities and Urban Management: IoT technologies are transforming cities into smart and sustainable ecosystems. Smart city applications include intelligent traffic management, smart parking systems, waste management optimization, and environmental monitoring. IoT sensors and data analytics enable efficient resource allocation, improved urban planning, and enhanced quality of life for citizens.

- ❖ Industrial Automation and Robotics: IoT-driven industrial automation and robotics are reshaping manufacturing, logistics, and supply chain operations. IoT-enabled machinery, robotics, and autonomous vehicles enhance production efficiency, enable predictive maintenance, and optimize logistics processes. IoT data analytics and machine learning algorithms enhance quality control, optimize production schedules, and enable real-time decision-making in industrial environments.

- ❖ Personalized IoT Experiences: IoT technologies are evolving to deliver personalized and context-aware experiences. By leveraging AI, machine learning, and data analytics, IoT systems can tailor services, recommendations, and interactions based on individual preferences, behavior patterns, and contextual information. This opens up possibilities for personalized healthcare, targeted marketing, and adaptive smart home environments.

These emerging applications and potential disruptions in the IoT landscape hold great promise for transforming industries, improving efficiency, and enhancing quality of life. As IoT continues to evolve and converge with other technologies, such as AI, 5G, and edge computing, the possibilities for innovation and disruption are expanding exponentially. Embracing these opportunities and addressing associated challenges will shape the future of IoT, leading to a more connected, intelligent, and sustainable world.

Conclusion

A. Recap of Key Points Discussed Throughout the Book

In this book, we embarked on a journey through the fascinating world of the Internet of Things (IoT) and explored its impact on our lives, industries, and society. Let's recap some of the key points we discussed throughout the book:

- ❖ Definition and Importance of IoT: We began by defining IoT as a network of interconnected physical devices that communicate and exchange data, enabling seamless integration between the digital and physical worlds. We explored the importance of IoT in transforming industries, improving efficiency, and enhancing our daily lives.

- ❖ Evolution of IoT: We delved into the historical background and origins of IoT, tracing its evolution from the early concepts of machine-to-machine communication to the interconnected world of today. We discussed the technological advancements that enabled the growth of IoT, including wireless connectivity, miniaturized sensors, and the increasing affordability of computing power.

❖ Core Components of IoT: We explored the core components of IoT, including sensors and actuators that collect and act upon data from the physical world. We discussed the various types of sensors and their functionalities, as well as the crucial role of actuators in enabling IoT systems to perform actions based on the collected data.

❖ Connectivity in IoT: We examined the importance of connectivity in IoT systems, focusing on wireless communication protocols that facilitate seamless data transmission between devices. We discussed protocols such as Wi-Fi, Bluetooth, Zigbee, and cellular networks, as well as the network infrastructures that support IoT deployments.

❖ Data Management and Analytics: We explored the challenges and considerations related to data management in IoT, including data collection, storage, and analytics. We discussed the importance of robust data security measures and the role of data analytics in extracting valuable insights from the vast amount of data generated by IoT devices.

❖ Applications of IoT: We delved into various applications of IoT across different domains. We discussed how IoT is transforming smart homes and home automation, enhancing security, and enabling energy management. We explored its impact on industrial sectors through automation, optimization, and predictive maintenance. We also examined its role in shaping smart cities and revolutionizing healthcare with remote patient monitoring and personalized healthcare solutions.

❖ Challenges and Considerations in IoT: We acknowledged the challenges and considerations associated with IoT, including security and privacy concerns. We highlighted the importance of addressing threats, vulnerabilities, and implementing strategies to secure IoT devices and data. We also discussed the need for interoperability, standardization, and ethical considerations to ensure a sustainable and inclusive IoT ecosystem.

❖ Future Trends and Possibilities: Lastly, we explored the future trends and possibilities in IoT. We discussed the role of emerging technologies such as artificial intelligence (AI) and machine learning in enhancing the capabilities of IoT systems. We explored the potential of edge computing and fog computing in reducing latency, optimizing bandwidth, and enabling real-time decision-making. We also discussed the transformative potential of 5G networks and next-generation technologies in expanding the possibilities of IoT.

Throughout this book, we have witnessed the tremendous impact of IoT on our world, from improving efficiency and productivity to revolutionizing industries and transforming the way we live. While IoT presents challenges, the possibilities and benefits it brings are vast. As we move forward, it is crucial to embrace the opportunities, address the challenges, and ensure that IoT is harnessed responsibly to create a connected, intelligent, and sustainable future for all.

B. Reflection on the Transformative Power of IoT

As we come to the end of this book exploring the Internet of Things (IoT), it is impossible not to be in awe of its transformative power. IoT has emerged as a game-changer, revolutionizing the way we interact with technology, businesses operate, and societies function. Let's reflect on the transformative power of IoT that we have witnessed throughout this journey:

- ❖ Connectivity and Integration: IoT has connected the world around us like never before. It has bridged the gap between physical and digital realms, enabling seamless integration between devices, systems, and people. This connectivity has fostered unprecedented opportunities for collaboration, innovation, and efficiency.

- ❖ Efficiency and Optimization: IoT has unleashed new levels of efficiency and optimization across industries. By collecting and analyzing vast amounts of data, IoT has enabled smarter decision-making, improved resource allocation, and enhanced operational efficiency. From supply chain management to manufacturing processes, IoT has brought about unprecedented levels of optimization and cost savings.

❖ Enhanced Experiences: IoT has transformed our everyday experiences, making them more convenient, personalized, and immersive. Smart homes that adapt to our preferences, wearable devices that monitor our health, and personalized recommendations based on our preferences are just a few examples of how IoT has elevated our daily lives.

❖ Empowering Industries: IoT has empowered industries to innovate and reimagine their operations. From healthcare to agriculture, IoT has revolutionized processes, enabling remote monitoring, predictive maintenance, and data-driven decision-making. It has empowered businesses to become more agile, responsive, and customer-centric.

❖ Enabling Sustainability: IoT has played a vital role in promoting sustainability and environmental stewardship. By optimizing energy usage, improving resource management, and enabling smarter transportation systems, IoT has contributed to reducing waste, conserving resources, and creating a more sustainable future.

❖ Empowering Individuals: IoT has empowered individuals to take control of their lives and well-being. Through wearable devices and health monitoring systems, individuals can track their fitness, manage chronic conditions, and make informed decisions about their health. IoT has empowered individuals to be more proactive and engaged in their own well-being.

❖ Creating New Opportunities: IoT has opened up a world of new opportunities, spurring innovation and entrepreneurship. Startups and businesses have leveraged the power of IoT to create novel products, services, and business models. The growth of the IoT ecosystem has created a fertile ground for collaboration, disruption, and economic growth.

❖ Global Impact: IoT has had a global impact, transcending boundaries and making a difference in communities around the world. From improving access to healthcare in remote areas to enabling efficient infrastructure management in smart cities, IoT has the potential to address pressing global challenges and bridge societal gaps.

As we conclude this exploration of IoT, it is evident that its transformative power knows no bounds. While we have discussed the opportunities and challenges, it is important to remember that responsible adoption and implementation of IoT are crucial. Ensuring data security, privacy, and ethical considerations should be at the forefront of our endeavors.

As IoT continues to evolve, it will reshape industries, revolutionize economies, and empower individuals. It is up to us to harness its potential for the greater good, keeping in mind the need for inclusivity, sustainability, and collaboration. Let us embrace the transformative power of IoT and work towards creating a connected, intelligent, and prosperous future for all.

C. Final Thoughts on the Future of Connected Technology

As we conclude this exploration of the Internet of Things (IoT) and connected technology, it is clear that we are at the precipice of a revolutionary era. The future holds immense potential for connected technology to shape our lives, industries, and societies in unprecedented ways. Here are some final thoughts on the future of connected technology:

❖ Ubiquitous Connectivity: We can expect connectivity to become even more pervasive in the future. With the advent of 5G networks, satellite constellations, and advancements in wireless communication technologies, virtually every device and location will be seamlessly connected. This ubiquitous connectivity will pave the way for innovative applications and transformative experiences across various domains.

❖ Intelligent Automation: Connected technology, combined with artificial intelligence (AI) and machine learning, will lead to intelligent automation on a massive scale. Machines and devices will learn from data, make informed decisions, and perform tasks autonomously. This will revolutionize industries, optimize processes, and free up human resources for more creative and strategic endeavors.

❖ Hyper-Personalization: Connected technology will enable hyper-personalization, tailoring experiences and services to individual preferences and needs. By leveraging data and analytics, connected devices will understand and adapt to our behaviors, providing personalized recommendations, anticipatory assistance, and immersive experiences that cater to our unique tastes and requirements.

❖ Digital Twins and Simulations: The concept of digital twins, virtual replicas of physical entities, will become increasingly prevalent. These digital counterparts will enable simulation, testing, and optimization of real-world scenarios, improving decision-making, reducing risks, and enhancing efficiency across industries. Digital twins will serve as invaluable tools for designing, monitoring, and optimizing complex systems and processes.

❖ Augmented Reality (AR) and Virtual Reality (VR): Connected technology will integrate seamlessly with AR and VR, creating immersive experiences that blend the physical and virtual worlds. AR and VR will enhance communication, training, education, entertainment, and collaboration, transforming the way we interact, learn, and experience the world around us.

❖ Ethical Considerations: As connected technology evolves, ethical considerations will play a crucial role. We must ensure data privacy, security, and transparency while addressing issues such as algorithmic bias, responsible AI, and the social impact of connected technology. Ethical frameworks, regulations, and responsible innovation will guide us towards a future where connected technology benefits all of humanity.

- ❖ Collaboration and Ecosystems: Connected technology will thrive in ecosystems characterized by collaboration, interoperability, and open standards. Collaboration among industries, academia, policymakers, and technology providers will be essential to unlock the full potential of connected technology. Open platforms, APIs, and partnerships will foster innovation and drive the development of comprehensive solutions.

- ❖ Sustainable and Resilient Systems: The future of connected technology must be built on sustainability and resilience. From energy-efficient devices and eco-friendly manufacturing processes to resilient networks and responsible end-of-life management, sustainability should be at the core of connected technology. Creating a circular economy and minimizing the environmental impact of connected devices will be imperative.

In conclusion, the future of connected technology is both thrilling and challenging. As we embrace the potential of IoT, 5G, AI, and other emerging technologies, it is essential to keep in mind the ethical, societal, and environmental considerations that come with this transformative power. By fostering collaboration, prioritizing sustainability, and upholding ethical principles, we can shape a future where connected technology enriches our lives, empowers industries, and creates a more connected, intelligent, and inclusive world for generations to come.

www.ingramcontent.com/pod-product-compliance
Lightning Source LLC
Chambersburg PA
CBHW071609270726
48661CB00019B/1666